Ripley's Believe It or Not!®

Developed and produced by Ripley Publishing Ltd

This edition published and distributed by:

Mason Crest
450 Parkway Drive, Suite D, Broomall, PA 19008
www.masoncrest.com

Printed and bound in the United States of America

First printing
9 8 7 6 5 4 3 2 1

Ripley's Believe It or Not!
Hard To Believe
ISBN: 978-1-4222-3143-2 (hardback)
Ripley's Believe It or Not!—Complete 8 Title Series
ISBN: 978-1-4222-3138-8

Cataloging-in-Publication Data is on file with the Library of Congress

PUBLISHER'S NOTE
While every effort has been made to verify the accuracy of the entries in this book, the Publishers cannot be held responsible for any errors contained in the work. They would be glad to receive any information from readers.

WARNING
Some of the stunts and activities in this book are undertaken by experts and should not be attempted by anyone without adequate training and supervision.

Ripley's Believe It or Not!®

Dare To Look

HARD TO BELIEVE

www.MasonCrest.com

HARD TO BELIEVE

Unbelievable tales. You really won't believe the remarkable stories inside this book. Be amazed by the mucky mud run, the skateboarding cat, and the incredible museum for ventriloquist dummies!

Camilla the rubber chicken floated to the edge of space in March 2012...

CHANGING FACES

Creative Director Dominick Reed from Cambridge, England, transformed his face every day for two whole years to create a series of wacky self-portraits, using a mix of computer wizardry, makeup, wigs, and props.

Better known to his online fans as his alter ego, Mr. Flibble, Dominick spent a total of 3,650 hours compiling his pictorial portfolio, and usually needed two to three hours a day to prepare for each picture, although it once took him an entire day when he had to bury himself in compost in his living room. Mr. Flibble often finds himself in strange predicaments, such as unlocking the secrets in his head, growing mustaches from his eyes, or getting addicted to laughter pills at clown school. He has such a large Internet following that, despite the crazy disguises, Mr. Flibble/Dominick gets recognized in the street!

THLY
Daily, for 27 years
Only £67
9 0123456789
438 PHOTOS
Matron's Raunchy
LAUGHTER
60
DO NOT SWALLOW
MAY CONTAIN NUTS

CHESS PIECE The Chess Club and Scholastic Center of St. Louis, Missouri, unveiled a king chess piece that was 14½ ft (4.4 m) tall and 6 ft (1.8 m) wide at the base—45 times larger than a standard chess piece.

BALLOON RUN Rob Ginnivan ran a half marathon while in a hot-air balloon high in the sky above Canberra, Australia. He ran the 13 mi (21 km) on a treadmill powered by a small generator inside the basket and finished in 2 hours 18 minutes.

QUICK KICKER Kickboxer Raul Meza, 33, of Sioux Falls, South Dakota, completed 335 martial arts kicks in a minute with one leg in November 2011. He once performed more than 18,000 kicks in a single eight-week period.

BABE AUCTION A New York Yankees jersey worn by Babe Ruth around 1920 sold for $4.42 million at an auction in California in 2012. At the same auction, his 1934 cap sold for $537,278 and one of his 1920s bats went for $591,007.

MUD RUN

Covered from head to toe in thick muck, a bearded athlete battles his way through the 2012 Bluegrass Mud Run, staged over a grueling 3-mi (5-km) course in Lexington, Kentucky. The mud is more than waist-deep in places and to make it even tougher, the competitors also have to crawl through the swamp beneath low obstacles.

HOT WHEELS▸ In an incredible life-sized Hot Wheels stunt, Team Hot Wheels drivers Greg Tracy and Tanner Foust raced two vehicles through a six-story double vertical loop at the 2012 X Games in Los Angeles, California, in June 2012. At speeds of more than 50 mph (80 km/h), they defied gravity and felt about 7Gs of g-force—the same as jet pilots experience in flight. During the stunt Foust had to make grunting noises to stop himself from blacking out.

WRONG COUNTRY▸ More than 400 Spanish soccer fans heading to the 2012 Europa League final landed in the wrong country after mixing up the names of two cities. The confused Athletic Bilbao supporters ended up in Budapest, Hungary—hundreds of miles away from the match in Bucharest, Romania.

BALL CATCHER▸ Zack Hample of New York City has caught more than 6,000 home-run and foul baseballs from Major League baseball games in over 50 different stadiums. In July 2012, he even caught a baseball dropped from a helicopter hovering 762 ft (232 m) above LeLacheur Park in Lowell, Massachusetts.

SKI CRAZY▸ Rainer Hertrich, a German-born snowcat operator at Copper Mountain, Colorado, skied every single day for 2,993 straight days—that's more than eight years. In that time he covered 98 million vertical ft (30 million m). He finally stopped on January 10, 2012, after he was diagnosed with a dangerously irregular heartbeat.

SOLITARY SQUID▸ A total of 74 competitors took part in the 2012 All England Squid Championship in Brighton, England, but at the end of five hours they had managed to catch only one squid between them—and that was just 0.4 in (1 cm) long. Nevertheless, it was enough for Davide Thambithurai to win the title for the second year running.

KENYAN MONOPOLY▸ Since 1968, a Kenyan athlete has won the men's 3,000-meter steeplechase every time the country has competed in the Olympics. At the London 2012 summer Olympics, Kenya won gold for the eighth time in a row and has now won 10 of the last 12 steeplechases, missing out only in 1976 and 1980 when the nation boycotted the Games.

THERE CAN BE UP TO 500 DIMPLES ON A REGULATION GOLF BALL.

PIGEON TRIANGLE▸ A small area of England has been dubbed the Bermuda Triangle of pigeon racing after hundreds of birds mysteriously vanished during races in 2012. In one event, only 13 out of 232 birds released in Thirsk, North Yorkshire, made it back to their homes in Scotland.

LONG STRIDES▸ It took Jamaica's Usain Bolt just 41 strides to break the Olympic men's 100-meters record with a time of just 9.63 seconds at the 2012 Olympic Games. Bolt's fellow countryman and Olympic silver medalist Yohan Blake took 46 strides to run the same distance.

YOUNGEST RACER▸ Stock car driver Braden DuBois from Indian River, Michigan, raced his Chevrolet four-cylinder car at Onaway Speedway for a full season at age nine, making him the world's youngest ever stock car racer.

TRICK SHOT▸ New York City chef Antony Riniti successfully performed a trick shot with 75 pool balls racked in triangles 25 stories high, making a tower more than 5 ft (1.5 m) tall. He carried out the trick by hitting the cue ball to pocket one of the balls at the base of the tower without the structure falling down.

TWIN RUNNERS▸ Identical twins Kevin and Jonathan Borlee of Belgium both reached the men's 400-meter final at the 2012 Olympics. Although split by the width of the track, they finished fifth and sixth respectively, separated by just 0.02 seconds.

NO REST▸ Seventeen-year-old U.S. swimmer Missy Franklin won gold in the women's 100-meters backstroke at the 2012 London Olympics less than 20 minutes after swimming in the 200-meters freestyle semi-final and qualifying for the final.

BULGING BICEPS

▸ New York City bodybuilder Gregg Valentino has biceps that measure a gigantic 28 in (71 cm) in circumference, making his arms larger than some people's waist. A bodybuilder since the age of 14, Gregg uses his mighty muscles to bicep-curl 300 lb (136 kg) and bench-press 550 lb (250 kg).

There's a place in Fort Mitchell, Kentucky, where old ventriloquist dummies go to retire.

Vent Haven

Believe it or not, the Vent Haven Museum is the world's only ventriloquism museum, and is home to thousands of artifacts and around 800 dummies.

Cecil Wigglenose

Created around 1938, Cecil Wigglenose has a nose that wiggles, eyes that cross, ears that twitch, eyebrows that move, a tongue that sticks out, and a fright wig. Made by the famous McElroy brothers, he is the only McElroy figure in the Vent Haven collection that is regularly demonstrated today.

The inside of Cecil Wigglenose's head shows the intricate workings that were the trademark of ventriloquists' doll makers George and Glenn McElroy. The typewriter-like mechanisms allowed their creations a full range of facial expressions.

The World of Vent Haven

The Vent Haven Museum houses the world's biggest collection of ventriloquists' figures—around 800—ranging in height from 4-in (10-cm) miniatures to 5½-ft (1.7-m) life-size dolls that can walk. The oldest wooden doll at Vent Haven dates back to 1820, and some of the early models have glass eyes, human hair, and real teeth—"accessories" that could be bought from barbershops.

Vent Haven was founded by William Shakespeare ("W.S.") Berger, who was a great lover of vaudeville. On a business trip to New York City in 1910, he bought his first figure, Tommy Baloney, so that he could try ventriloquism for himself. However, his interest wore off, and Tommy Baloney was put in storage for 20 years until Berger pulled him out to perform at a Christmas party at the Cincinnati tile factory where he worked.

The act went down so well that Berger began collecting ventriloquism memorabilia and soon dummies filled his house—before long he had to construct a second building in his backyard. Berger became President of the International Brotherhood of Ventriloquism from the late 1940s, and when he died in 1972, aged 94, his attorney helped to turn his private collection into a public museum—Vent Haven opened in 1974.

W.S. Berger with Tommy Baloney. Created by Louis Grannat in 1910, Tommy Baloney was the first of hundreds of figures owned by Berger and the one that inspired the whole Vent Haven collection.

The Early Days

Ventriloquism first became popular in vaudeville in the late 19th century. Early dummies were often made of papier-mâché, had a string-and-loop system that operated the head and mouth, and manually controlled eyebrows. Later, eyebrows were sometimes moved by weight control (moving the head) and internal controls were on a stick, often made from ordinary household items.

Performers, such as Englishman **Jules Vernon** (1867–1937), liked to demonstrate their ability at seamlessly switching voices by conducting running dialogue with as many as seven different puppet characters, both male and female (right). Another Englishman, **Fred Russell** (1862–1957), was the first ventriloquist to have a single figure perched on his knee, a style copied by **The Great Lester** (1878–1956) (below), who is credited with developing the wooden dummy.

One of Lester's pupils was **Edgar Bergen,** who, with his doll **Charlie McCarthy,** starred throughout the golden age of ventriloquism—the 1930s and 1940s. Other performers of that era included **Max Terhune** and his puppet **Elmer,** who appeared together in western movies alongside a young John Wayne, and **Dick Bruno,** who spoke with a sophisticated French accent, while his doll, **Joe Flip,** wisecracked in a Brooklyn accent.

Jules Vernon went blind at age 53, but he never revealed this publicly. The characters for his act were mounted on a bench, from which his wife ran a thread to guide him on from backstage. Once there, he knew where the controls were and performed as if he could see.

This 1937 signed photo to W.S. Berger from The Great Lester reads, "a real friend of all ventriloquists and a real deep student of the complete art of ventriloquism."

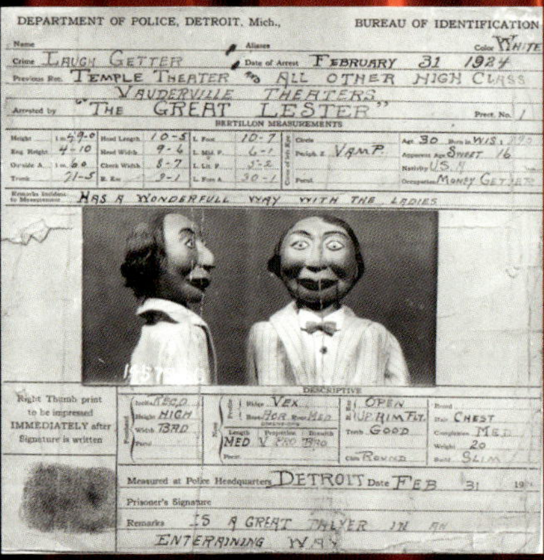

DEPARTMENT OF POLICE, DETROIT, Mich., BUREAU OF IDENTIFICATION

Color: WHITE

Crime: LAUGH GETTER — Date of Arrest: FEBRUARY 31 1924

Previous Rec.: TEMPLE THEATER & ALL OTHER HIGH CLASS VAUDEVILLE THEATERS

Arrested by: "THE GREAT LESTER" — Prect. No. 1

BERTILLON MEASUREMENTS

Age: 30 — Born in: WIS. — Apparent Age: SWEET 16 — Nativity: U.S.A. — Occupation: MONEY GETTER

Remarks Incident to Measurement: HAS A WONDERFULL WAY WITH THE LADIES

Right Thumb print to be impressed IMMEDIATELY after Signature is written

DESCRIPTIVE — Teeth: GOOD — Chest — Weight: 20 — Build: SLIM

Measured at Police Headquarters: DETROIT — Date: FEB 31 19

Prisoner's Signature

Remarks: IS A GREAT TALKER IN AN ENTERRAINING WAY

A fake police record card belonging to Frank Byron Jr., which lists his crime as "Laugh Getter" and remarks how he has "a wonderful way with the ladies."

The Great Lester & Frank Byron Jr.

Born Maryan Czajkowski, Lester used to drink a glass of water while his puppet, Frank Byron Jr., spoke. On one occasion, the show's musicians substituted whiskey for water as a prank. Lester downed the whiskey without any noticeable effect, but Frank started coughing and shaking as if he had drunk it! Lester also performed a routine where Frank blew out his matches while he tried to light a cigarette.

Behind the Scenes

Considerable work went into the creation of the dummies, some of which went on to achieve great success with their ventriloquist partners. The ingenuity and artistry of some of the dummy makers led to their work being in great demand.

George and Glenn McElroy worked as a team, with the elder brother, Glenn, doing the mechanics and George, a draughtsman by profession, concentrating on the artistic aspect, including the sculpting of the heads, painting the faces, and hand-weaving the hair for the wigs.

The McElroys' figure Oscar was used by ventriloquist Harry Tunks who was a colonel in the U.S. Air Force. He performed shows after he retired from service after World War II.

The McElroy Brothers

George and Glenn McElroy of Harrison, Ohio, created the Rolls-Royces of ventriloquists' figures. Their dummies are generally considered to be the finest ever built, with a unique system of typewriter-like controls inside each one's body allowing for as many as 16 different facial functions.

McElroy figures could move their jaw, twitch their nose, curl their top lip, float their eyes from side to side, look down, cross their eyes, move their eyebrows, wink, stick out their tongue, wiggle their ears, and even raise their hair in fright. The dolls were given exaggerated facial expressions so that they could be seen by people sitting in the back row of the theater.

The McElroys made fewer than 50 ventriloquists' figures before retiring, including **Cecil Wigglenose, Skinny Dugan,** and **Oscar.** They also created a talking skull, a full-size human skull mounted on a short post and operated via a flatboard base, which the ventriloquist held.

For **W.S. Berger** they built **Jacko,** a 3-ft-tall (0.9-m) monkey whose body was covered in dyed rabbit fur and who had a movable upper lip made from a lady's kid glove.

Frank Marshall

Frank Marshall was the most famous and most prolific maker of ventriloquists' figures in history, carving hundreds of puppets, including such famous faces as **Danny O'Day, Jerry Mahoney,** and **Farfel.**

He owed his success to the Mack & Son Woodworking Shop in Chicago, which originally specialized in carving doorframes and ornamental signs until ventriloquist **The Great Lester** asked the Macks to make him a new figure for his act. When word got out, many other ventriloquists approached the Macks, and business boomed.

Frank Marshall kept refining his ventriloquist figures throughout his career, and today his creations are cherished by professionals and collectors alike. His human dolls are readily recognizable by their heavily lined eyes and smiling "cheeky boy" features.

After the Macks died, an industrial model maker named Alex Cameron purchased the shop. He didn't have the same skills as the Macks for making figures, so he hired Frank Marshall in 1925 to do the work. After a few years, Cameron contracted tuberculosis. Realizing he owed Marshall money for the work he had done making the figures, Cameron gave the business to Marshall as due payment.

One of Marshall's most ingenious models was **Champagne Charlie,** a life-sized walking figure made for **W.S. Berger** in 1938. Charlie had moving eyes, a smoking mechanism, and a walking cane.

Ventriloquist Jimmy Nelson with a range of puppets made by celebrated craftsman Frank Marshall. Left to right: Humphrey Higsbye, Danny O'Day, Farfel the dog, and Ftatateeta the cat.

Marshall tailored his hand-carved dolls to suit the personality and appearance of the ventriloquist. So when ventriloquist **Jimmy Nelson** asked Marshall to make him a figure, Marshall watched Nelson's theater act and came up with a dummy that Nelson called **Danny O'Day** because the name, unlike "McCarthy" and '"Mahoney," contained none of the consonants that ventriloquists struggle to say without moving their lips.

Marshall later made Nelson another figure, **Farfel** the dog, which had ears that pulled up. For ten years from 1955, Farfel was the face of Nestlé chocolate drink commercials, but Nelson's nerves nearly blew the audition. As Farfel sang the last word "chocolate," Nelson's hand slipped off the control, causing the dog's jaw to snap shut. Luckily the executives loved it, told Nelson to keep it in, and it became Farfel's trademark.

CHAMPAGNE CHARLIE

Created by Frank Marshall for W.S. Berger

Standing 5 ft 4 in (1.6 m) tall and built so that he could carry a cane, Charlie's walking mechanism was later remodeled by the McElroys as Berger struggled to master it.

JACKO

Created c.1940 by the McElroys for W.S. Berger

Berger paid $125 for Jacko, who has simultaneously curling upper and lower lips, a stick-out tongue, sniffing nose, moving and crossing eyes, and wiggling ears.

ROSITA

Created in 1943 by and for Bill Hume

Rosita was made in Panama out of wood salvaged from a torpedoed cargo ship during World War II. She switches effortlessly from Spanish to English, and was originally transported in a parachute bag.

PROFESSOR I.Q.

Created by Frank Marshall

The professor has a device at the hairline that enables him to sweat in times of stress or intense thought. His arm also raises, which looks as if he is saluting.

SKINNY DUGAN

Created by Fred and Madeleine Maher in the 1930s

Skinny can wiggle his ears, spit, and cry. He was the first professional model made by the Mahers. Fred used the model in the 1940s.

SKINNY HAMILTON

Created by Frank Marshall for W.S. Berger

Skinny has a fright wig, he cries, and his hands are carved to fit gloves. He was W.S. Berger's favorite figure.

Edgar Bergen ▶

Edgar Bergen was presented with an Honorary Oscar (in the form of a wooden Academy Award) for his creation of the inimitable Charlie McCarthy. An original wooden Charlie McCarthy is on permanent display at the Smithsonian Institution in Washington, D.C.

▶ *At Vent Haven there are dolls of Jimmy Carter and Ronald Reagan, as well as Mary Lou, who along with three other dummies was the sole survivor of a 1908 shipwreck that killed her owner, Will Wood, and every human on board (far right). In addition to endless rows of immaculately dressed dolls, the museum displays books on the subject dating back to the 1700s, plus more than 10,000 photographs and playbills.*

Skinny Hamilton ▼

Vent Haven founder W.S. Berger with his favorite figure, Skinny Hamilton. He said that if the museum were ever to fold, all the figures except Skinny should be sold and the proceeds given to charity. "Do not dispose of this figure as Skinny is part of me," he wrote, listing the dummy specifically in his will. In the final year of his life, he asked for Skinny to be brought to his nursing home where he proceeded to entertain nursing staff and his fellow patients.

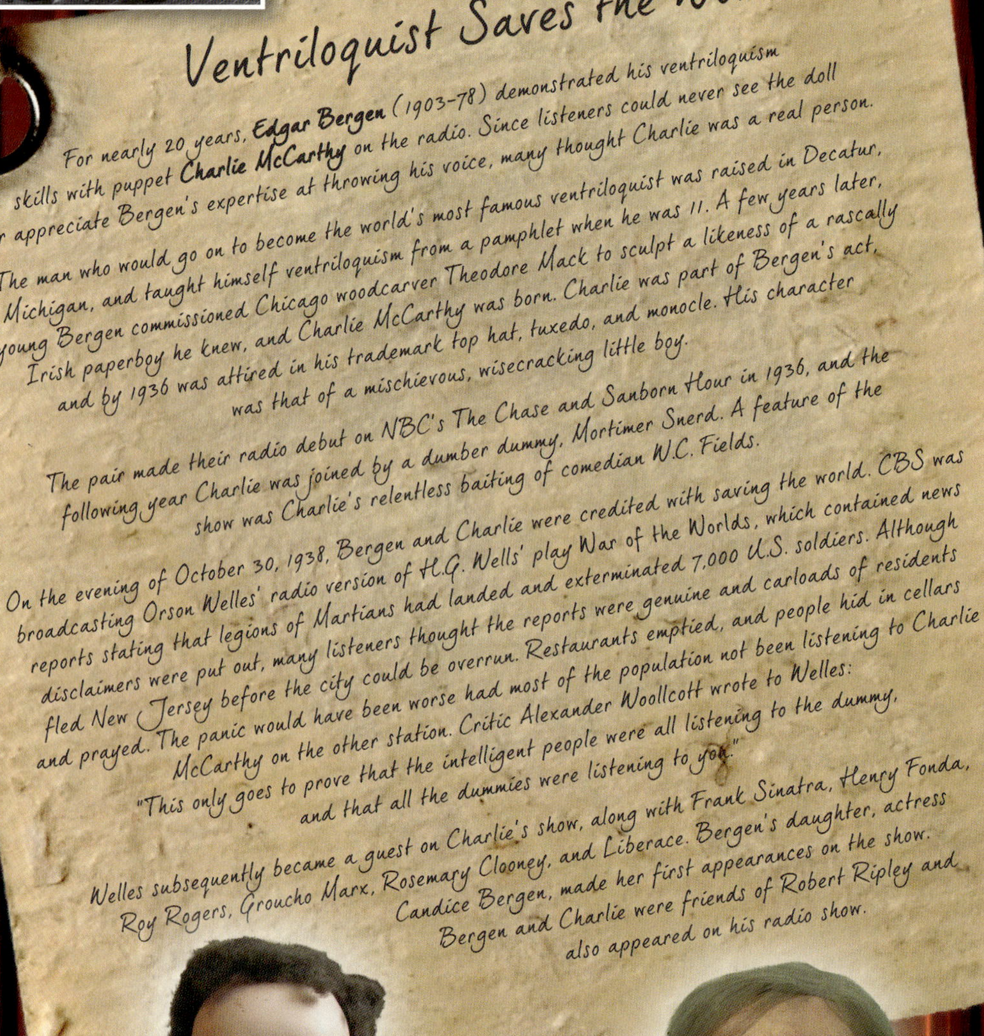

Ventriloquist Saves the World!

For nearly 20 years, **Edgar Bergen** (1903–78) demonstrated his ventriloquism skills with puppet **Charlie McCarthy** on the radio. Since listeners could never see the doll or appreciate Bergen's expertise at throwing his voice, many thought Charlie was a real person.

The man who would go on to become the world's most famous ventriloquist was raised in Decatur, Michigan, and taught himself ventriloquism from a pamphlet when he was 11. A few years later, young Bergen commissioned Chicago woodcarver Theodore Mack to sculpt a likeness of a rascally Irish paperboy he knew, and Charlie McCarthy was born. Charlie was part of Bergen's act, and by 1936 was attired in his trademark top hat, tuxedo, and monocle. His character was that of a mischievous, wisecracking little boy.

The pair made their radio debut on NBC's The Chase and Sanborn Hour in 1936, and the following year Charlie was joined by a dumber dummy, Mortimer Snerd. A feature of the show was Charlie's relentless baiting of comedian W.C. Fields.

On the evening of October 30, 1938, Bergen and Charlie were credited with saving the world. CBS was broadcasting Orson Welles' radio version of H.G. Wells' play War of the Worlds, which contained news reports stating that legions of Martians had landed and exterminated 7,000 U.S. soldiers. Although disclaimers were put out, many listeners thought the reports were genuine and carloads of residents fled New Jersey before the city could be overrun. Restaurants emptied, and people hid in cellars and prayed. The panic would have been worse had most of the population not been listening to Charlie McCarthy on the other station. Critic Alexander Woollcott wrote to Welles: "This only goes to prove that the intelligent people were all listening to the dummy, and that all the dummies were listening to you."

Welles subsequently became a guest on Charlie's show, along with Frank Sinatra, Henry Fonda, Roy Rogers, Groucho Marx, Rosemary Clooney, and Liberace. Bergen's daughter, actress Candice Bergen, made her first appearances on the show. Bergen and Charlie were friends of Robert Ripley and also appeared on his radio show.

JOE FLIP

Created in the 1940s by Frank Marshall

Considered by Marshall to be his masterpiece, Joe was originally called Brewster but was later renamed after saxophone player Flip Phillips.

OSCAR

Created by Mack & Son

Oscar was used by magician and ventriloquist Howard Kingsley (real name Herman Schanbacher), who lived from 1885 to 1939 and wrote a book on the art of ventriloquism.

MAX

Created by Ramme for Charlotte Bern-Keller

Max cries, smiles, nods, winks, rolls his eyes, lifts his eyebrows, moves his right arm and leg, and can smoke a cigarette. He always wore makeup for his shows.

Sole Survivors

When a tugboat carrying American Will Wood, who was billed at the time as the "World's Greatest Ventriloquist," sank in a storm in the Gulf of Mexico in 1908, the only survivors were four of his dummies—Woo Woo, Clown, Mary Lou, and Mike (below). Wood and his 20-year-old daughter Bertha perished in the tragedy, but his beloved figures washed ashore in Texas in a trunk and were taken to Wood's widow. She wanted nothing to do with them, however, and gave them to a friend of her husband's. Eventually, they were donated to Vent Haven.

Prison Dummy

This dummy at Vent Haven called Ruland was carved by German prisoner-of-war Erich Everty while he was being held in a Russian camp during World War II. He made the head from a scrap piece of firewood, and used tar for the eyes and newspapers for the body. Ruland's main purpose was to entertain the cooks in return for extra food.

Convertible Nurse

Believe it or not, this Vent Haven large nurse figure, manufactured in the 1900s and used by Canadian ventriloquist and professional whistler John A. Kelly, converts into a full-size grandfather clock!

JOHNNY

Created in the 1930s by the McElroys for George Pullin

Johnny has moving eyes and eyebrows, a stick-out tongue, a moving nose with a bulb and switch that allows the nose to light up, flapping ears, and a fright wig.

ELMER

Created by Frank Marshall for Max Terhune

Elmer, originally called Skully, adopted the name "Elmer Sneezeweed" after his first western. He appeared in more than 20 western movies during the 1930s and 1940s.

MAISIE

Created by Leonardo (Horatio M. Ortega) for himself

Maisie has a small pink balloon in her mouth that could be blown up using a bulb syringe so it looked like a bubble-gum bubble.

ANT ALERT A September 2011 high school football game between Hunter-Kinard-Tyler and Calhoun County at Neeses, South Carolina, was postponed because of fire ants. The referee found up to 20 large and active fire ant mounds on the field and despite attempts to dig them up and pour salt on them, the game had to be called off.

TRIPLE TIE Three greyhounds in a race in Essex, England, on January 19, 2011, made history by crossing the finish line in a triple dead heat, beating odds of many millions to one. Even the track's photo-finish technology was unable to separate them, and what made the three-way tie all the more remarkable was that the dogs were running over the maximum distance of 1,011 yd (925 m).

SURE SHOT Shooter Kimberley Rhode won the women's skeet gold medal at the London 2012 Summer Olympics to become the first U.S. competitor to win an individual shooting medal in five consecutive Olympics. She finished with 99 points, missing only one of the 100 clay targets she shot at all day.

POLE POSITION In the crazy Japanese sport of Bo-Taoshi, two teams of 75 players compete—one team defending a tall wooden pole while the other team tries to knock it down. By pulling, punching, grabbing, and kicking their opponents, the attackers have about 2½ minutes to lower the defending team's upright pole to an angle of 30 degrees or less. If they fail to do so, the defending team wins.

NO FEET Eleven-year-old Brazilian schoolboy Gabriel Muniz was invited to train with Spanish soccer giants Barcelona—even though he has no feet. Despite being born without feet, he is one of the best players at his school and impressed Barcelona chiefs when they saw his incredible ball skills on TV.

BROKEN LEG U.S. 4 x 400 meters relay runner Manteo Mitchell ran half of his race at the 2012 London Summer Olympics with a broken leg! He felt a bone snap partway through running the first leg of the relay, but he kept sprinting through the last 200 meters because he didn't want to let his team-mates down. Despite his injury, he still ran the 400 meters in 46.1 seconds and helped the United States to finish as joint-fastest qualifiers.

COW RACE

At the annual Pacu Jawi Cow Race in West Sumatra, Indonesia, jockeys ride pairs of cows along a muddy course while desperately hanging on to their mounts by their tails. To make the cows go faster, the jockeys bite their tails. The event, which dates back hundreds of years, was originally contested by farmers for relaxation at the start of the rice-harvesting season.

DRAG RACER Belle Wheeler from Northamptonshire, England, passed her drag-racing driving test becoming the world's youngest drag car racer—just one day after her eighth birthday. She has gone on to compete against drivers more than twice her age in her specially modified dragster, which can rocket from 0 to 50 mph (80 km/h) in just 12 seconds.

SUPER GIRL When she won the women's 400 meters individual medley at the 2012 Olympics, 16-year-old Chinese swimmer Ye Shiwen swam the last 50 meters faster than American Ryan Lochte covered the same distance in the corresponding men's race—the first time a woman had ever beaten a man's time at that stage of the race. Her total time of 4 minutes 28.23 seconds was so fast it would have won the men's gold medal at the Olympics in 1964, 1968, and 1972.

GENTLE OGRE

Maurice "The Angel" Tillet—seen here waving his official papers—became a citizen of the United States in 1947.

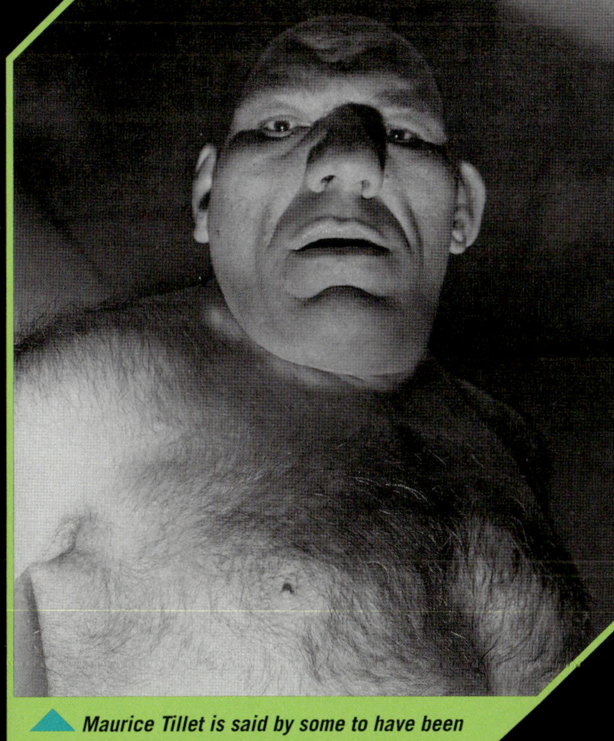

Maurice Tillet is said by some to have been the inspiration behind the movie character Shrek.

Maurice Tillet, a Russian-born French professional wrestler of the 1940s, was such a beautiful child that he was nicknamed "The Angel"—but when he was 17 he noticed a mysterious swelling in his feet, hands, and head and was diagnosed with acromegaly, a pituitary disorder that results in the abnormal growth of these areas.

Maurice could speak several languages and had wanted to become a lawyer, but his disfigurement prevented him doing so and instead he took up wrestling in the United States. He was known as "The French Angel" and "the freak ogre of the ring." His proportions—he weighed 280 lb (127 kg) and had huge hands and an oversized head but was a modest 5 ft 8½ in (1.74 m) tall—made him difficult to wrestle against and for many years he was billed as "unstoppable." A huge box office draw, Maurice was twice recognized as world heavyweight champion by the American Wrestling Association. He died in 1954, aged 50, a year after his last professional fight.

OLYMPIC YARN

An anonymous "yarnbomber" wrapped the town pier at Saltburn in North Yorkshire, England, with a 150-ft-long (46-m) scarf depicting woolen athletes competing in a variety of Olympic events, including synchronized swimming, rowing, weightlifting, and cycling.

SKATEBOARDING CAT

MODERN CAVEMAN Daniel Suelo has lived without money since giving it up in 2000. He left his last $30 in a phone booth and walked off into the wilderness, where he has lived in caves, stayed in communes, and camped outdoors. For several years he made his home in a vast cave on the edge of a cliff in the Arches National Park, Utah, where he carved a bed out of rock, foraged for food, drank from springs, and bathed in a nearby stream. He pays no taxes and accepts no financial help from the government.

SHARED GRAVE Archeologists excavating a 5th-century cemetery in Cambridgeshire, England, discovered the grave of a woman who had been buried with a cow. Male Anglo-Saxon warriors were sometimes buried with horses, but finding a woman sharing a grave with a cow was described by experts as "genuinely bizarre."

DECOY RESCUE Answering distress calls from members of the public, a team of 25 firefighters performed a hazardous nighttime rescue to save a swan stuck in a frozen pond in Straubing, Germany, only to find that the bird was a plastic decoy put there by fishermen to scare away other birds.

HOT HEAD

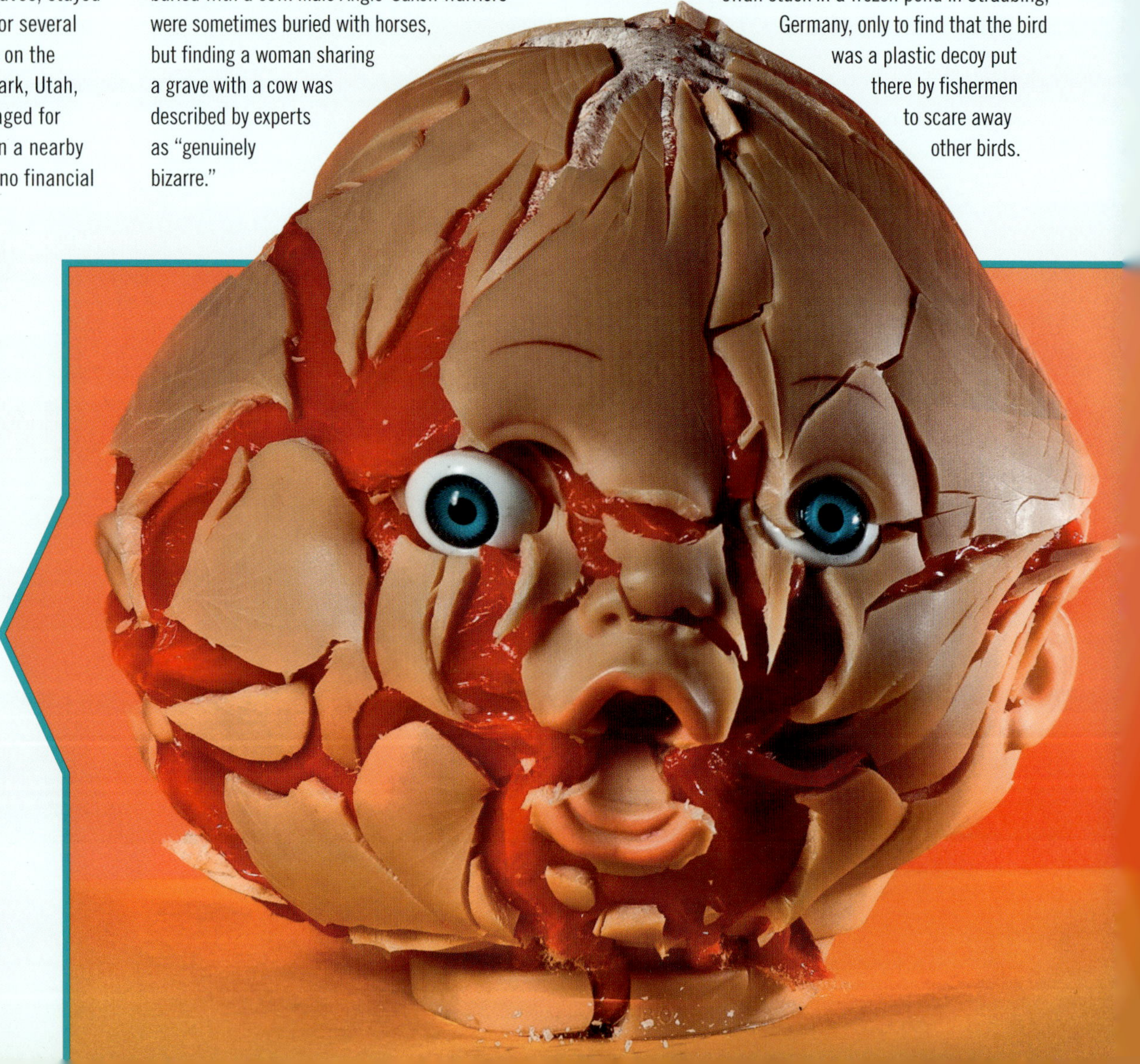

Alan Sailer, a photographer from California, has created twisted versions of popular Christmas gifts, dolls, and toys by blowing them up and capturing the carnage with very high-speed photography. This head is filled with red gelatin, and the explosion is courtesy of a firecracker concealed within the toy and electronically controlled. Do not try it at home!

Romeo, a male purebred Bengal cat from Seattle, Washington, has learned to skateboard! He puts all four paws on the board to ride around the house. Romeo can also jump through hoops, leap over hurdles, give a high-five, walk backward on his hind legs, and play a cat-sized piano.

CAT MAYOR In 2012, Stubbs, a cat with no tail, celebrated his 15th year as mayor of Talkeetna, Alaska, making him one of the longest-serving mayors in the United States. He has more than 1,000 friends on Facebook, which is 100 more than the town's entire population.

SLEEPING ZOMBIE On the morning of November 1, 2012, a passerby called police in Birmingham, Alabama, after seeing what looked like a woman shot dead in her car and slumped over the steering wheel—but when officers arrived, they actually found a drunken Halloween reveler who had passed out wearing a zombie costume splattered with fake blood.

SMUGGLED FRIEND A man convicted of smuggling in Sweden outsmarted his jailers by sneaking in a friend to serve most of his one-year sentence. The replacement convict arrived with a driving license in the smuggler's name but bearing his own photograph. The deception was discovered only when he was released on probation after serving two-thirds of his friend's sentence.

DEAD BEDMATE After his wife died in 2003, Le Van of Quang Nam, Vietnam, was so upset that he slept on top of her grave for 20 months. When the wind and rain finally became unbearable, he excavated a tunnel into the grave, dug her up, wrapped her bones in gypsum, dressed her, put a dummy mask on her face, and has slept in bed next to her ever since.

RITUAL SURGERY In 2011, Simon Eroro, a journalist in Papua New Guinea, traveled into the jungle and, as part of a ritual cleansing ceremony, agreed to be circumcised with bamboo sticks just to get an interview with a group of rebels.

TIP OFF An armed robber fled with money from the cash register of a store in Albuquerque, New Mexico, but left behind a piece of his finger.

COFFIN CLASS Randy Schnobrich, a woodworker from Grand Marais, Minnesota, teaches a "Build Your Own Coffin" class for those who want to be buried in their own handiwork.

WHEELY CRAZY Drew Beaumier from Fountain Valley, California, has turned himself into a real-life Transformer. By designing a hinged robot costume with wheels on the arms and legs, he can fold into car form and "drive" along the street. Then when he stands up, the outfit opens into an Optimus Prime pose. He made the costume in eight weeks by dismantling a toy car, reassembling the parts with hinges, and gluing it to a sports undergarment so that he can wear it like a suit.

LOUDEST PURR Smokey, a cat owned by Ruth Adams of Northampton, England, has the world's loudest purr, officially measured at 67.7 decibels, but she has also been known to purr at 92 decibels, equivalent to the noise of a lawn mower, a hair dryer, or a Boeing 737 coming in to land. Most cats purr at around 25 decibels, but Smokey's deafening sounds make it difficult for anyone to hear the TV or radio if she is in the room.

TOWN SOLD

In 2012, Buford, Wyoming, was sold for $900,000 to a buyer from Vietnam after the town's sole resident and owner since 1992, Don Sammons, decided to move to Colorado to be nearer his son. Buford was once home to 2,000 people, but in recent years Sammons was the only resident for miles around—although 1,000 visitors a day did descend on the place in summer, curious to see the town with a population of one.

FAT FIRE The burning fat from an obese corpse caused a fire that almost destroyed a crematorium in Graz, Austria. The fire started when large amounts of burning fat from a 440-lb (200-kg) woman's body blocked an air filter, leading the system to overheat.

HANGING ON Traffic policeman Second Lieutenant Nguyen Manh Phan clung for more than half a mile to the windshield wipers of a bus traveling at 30 mph (48 km/h) through the streets of Hanoi, Vietnam, after the bus driver sped off before he could be ticketed.

BACON COFFIN A food company based in Seattle, Washington State, has created a $3,000 coffin painted in a bacon design.

BIG BANG Instead of the planned 30 minutes' entertainment for a crowd of hundreds of people, a 2011 Community Fireworks Display in Oban, Scotland, lasted only one minute after a technical hitch resulted in all of the fireworks going off at once.

MOBY SICK

While walking on a beach in Dorset, England, eight-year-old Charlie Naysmith discovered a 21-oz (600-g) piece of whale vomit that is worth up to $60,000. Sperm whale vomit that has solidified over time into a waxy substance is called ambergris or "floating gold" and is valuable because it is used in expensive perfumes to prolong the scent.

HAND GRENADE Students were evacuated from a school in Newcastle, New South Wales, Australia, in 2012 when an 11-year-old brought a hand grenade to class for show-and-tell. The children were taken to a nearby park while police and bomb appraisal technicians examined the inactive World War II grenade.

TURTLE RECALL In 1965, 13-year-old Jeff Cokeley carved his initials and the date into the shell of a box turtle he found on his family's farm in southwestern Pennsylvania—and 47 years later his father Holland was walking a dog on the farm when he stumbled across the same turtle with its markings still in place.

MOVING KISS After their wedding in Yuxi, China, bride and groom Li Wen and Lu Ben exchanged the traditional kiss—while sitting in different moving cars. The newlyweds traveled in separate vehicles to the reception, and on the way the drivers inched close together so that the couple could wind down their windows and share a kiss on the highway.

CRAZY THIEF While trying to break into an electrical substation, Michael Harper of Leicester, England, suffered serious burns and knocked out the power to 2,000 homes when he urinated on a transformer.

IN PIECES A mentally ill woman in Sichuan, China, tore up 50,000 yuan (about $8,000) in bank notes. Her husband took the scraps to the bank where 12 members of staff worked for six hours trying to piece them back together, but in that time they managed to complete just one.

- Erika La Tour Eiffel from San Francisco, California, married the Eiffel Tower because she had fallen hopelessly in love with the French landmark.
- Chen Wei-yih from Taipei, Taiwan, married herself to demonstrate how happy she was in her own company.
- Korean Lee Jin-gyu married a pillow decorated with a picture of his favorite female animated character, Fate Testarossa.
- In Possendorf, Germany, Uwe Mitzscherlich married his cat Cecilia after being told that his pet did not have long to live.
- Two-year-old Sagula Munda was married to a dog at a ceremony in Jaipur, India, to protect the boy from further bad luck after he contracted a rotten tooth.
- Sharon Tendler married Cindy the dolphin at a special ceremony in Eilat, Israel. Cindy was rewarded with a kiss and a piece of herring.

DONKEY WEDDING

At a festival in Zamora, Spain, to celebrate Saint Anthony, the patron saint of animals, groom Isidro Fernandez Rodriguez chose as his beautiful bride his donkey Matilde.

PARTY TIME▸ Over 140 political parties contested the 2010 U.K. general election, including the Fancy Dress Party, the Monster Raving Loony Party, the Nobody Party, the Pirate Party, and the Bus Pass Elvis Party.

ACCIDENTAL MAYOR▸ Fabio Borsatti became mayor of Cimolais, Italy, after running for office only to help his friend, Gino Bertolo, the one other candidate, who did not want to stand unopposed.

VAMPIRE SKELETONS▸ Bulgarian archeologists discovered two 800-year-old "vampire" skeletons during excavations near the Black Sea. The two men had been stabbed through the stomach and chest with iron rods as part of a ritual designed to prevent them turning into vampires after death.

GORILLA DUMPED▸ A 15-ft-high (4.5-m) metal gorilla statue was found mysteriously dumped on a path in Cambridgeshire, England, in March 2012. Enforcement officers described it as the most unusual case of illegal dumping they had known.

MASS WEDDING▸ In March 2012, 2,000 couples from 54 countries attended a mass wedding at a stadium in Gapyeong, South Korea.

TWICE LUCKY▸ Virginia Fike of Berryville, Virginia, won two Powerball lotteries on the same day—April 7, 2012—winning a total of $2 million.

BEST DOG▸ When Sue and Michael Hopkins got married in Swansea, Wales, their 11-year-old lurcher dog Snoopy was their best man. The dog kept the rings in a bag around his neck and barked to let guests know that the service had finished.

WRAP ARTISTS

▸ Wes Naman from Albuquerque, New Mexico, is a photographer who has created a series of distorted portraits by wrapping his friends' faces in sticky tape. He had the idea for his Scotch Tape Series *after applying tape to himself to test a lighting rig set-up—and was so impressed by the weird, zombie-like results that he encouraged more than 30 of his friends to have their noses, lips, ears, and eyebrows temporarily twisted.*

TALL PEOPLE

Only 17 people in history are known to have reached a height of 8 ft (2.4 m) or more—and measuring 8 ft 11.1 in (2.72 m) from head to toe, Robert Wadlow (1918–40) was the tallest man ever to have lived. Even today's contenders for the title of world's tallest person don't come anywhere near his great height. Known as the "Alton Giant," after his hometown of Alton, Illinois, Robert wore size 37 shoes that cost $100 a pair—equivalent to $1,500 today—and he traveled everywhere in a car that had the passenger seat removed so that he could sit in the back and stretch his long legs.

When he died from an infection, aged 22, Wadlow was buried in a specially made 10-ft-6-in-long (3.2-m) steel coffin that was interred in a vault of solid concrete because his family feared that his body might be stolen. Like most excessively tall people, he had suffered from an over-active pituitary gland, which resulted in an abnormally high level of human growth hormone.

Weighing 356 lb (162 kg) and standing 7 ft 4 in (2.23 m) tall, New Jersey-born Aurelio "Al" Tomaini (1912–62) spent most of his adult life as a circus performer despite taking medication to curb his growth. While appearing in Cleveland in 1936, he met his future wife Jeanie—the "Half Girl"—who was born with no legs and stood just 2 ft 6 in (76 cm) tall. They toured for years as the "World's Strangest Married Couple," with Al usually propping Jeanie on his shoulder or carrying her at his side.

Although he was a normal-sized baby, Robert Wadlow grew so fast that even at elementary school they had to make a special desk for him. He was 6 ft (1.8 m) tall by age eight and when he joined the Boy Scouts at 13 he stood 7 ft 4 in (2.2 m) tall. It required 14 yd (13 m) of 3-ft-wide (1-m) material to make his uniform. When he died aged only 22, he was still growing, so he would almost certainly have become the only person ever to stand over 9 ft (2.74 m) tall.

Raised in Willow Bunch, Saskatchewan, Canada, and the oldest of 20 children, Edouard Beaupré (1881–1904) wanted to be a cowboy but was so tall that his legs were too long for him to ride even the tallest of horses comfortably. Instead, he toured with sideshows as the "Willow Bunch Giant," wrestling strongmen and performing incredible feats of strength. His most celebrated stunt was crouching beneath a 900-lb (408-kg) horse and lifting it up on his shoulders. When he died he was 8 ft 3 in (2.51 m) tall and his body was embalmed and displayed at a Montreal circus until the city's university acquired it for research into abnormal growth. In 1990, 86 years after his death, Beaupré was finally laid to rest and cremated.

Born in Letcher County, Kentucky, Martin Van Buren Bates (1837–1919) became known as the "Kentucky Giant" after a sudden growth spurt sent his height rocketing to 7 ft 9 in (2.36 m). He was a captain in the Confederate Army during the Civil War, his size prompting Union soldiers to tell tales of a "Confederate giant who's as big as five men and fights like 50." After the war, he joined a circus where he met 7-ft-5-in-tall (2.27-m) Anna Haining Swan, and in 1871 the couple married in London, England, drawing a crowd of thousands to witness "the wedding of the giants."

John Rogan (1868–1905) from Sumner County, Tennessee, was the second tallest person in history, growing to a height of 8 ft 8 in (2.64 m). He underwent a rapid growth spurt at age 13, which eventually left him unable to stand or walk. So he got around by converting his bed into a cart, which was pulled by goats. Rogan, whose hands were 11 in (28 cm) long, earned a living by selling portraits and postcards of himself at a train station.

Welshman George Auger (1881–1922) started out as a policeman but, because of his 7-ft-5-in (2.26-m) size, he created a disturbance wherever he went. It was said that there was enough cloth in one of his suits to fit out an entire family. At 5 ft 4 in (1.6 m), his wife Bertha often used a ladder to kiss him and was afraid to sit on his lap for fear of falling off. When the couple went to see the Barnum & Bailey Circus, Auger found that he stood a full head taller than the show's giant and was hired and given the name the "Cardiff Giant," going on to tour the United States as a circus performer. In 1922, Auger was asked by comedy star Harold Lloyd to appear in the silent movie Why Worry?, but unfortunately he died shortly after filming began.

Standing 7ft 6½ in (2.3 m) tall, singer and actor William Olding was hailed as the tallest man in England in the 1930s. When he appeared as an angel in a 1936 play, more than 19½ yd (18 m) of cloth were required to make his costume and the dressmaker had to climb a stepladder to reach his shoulders.

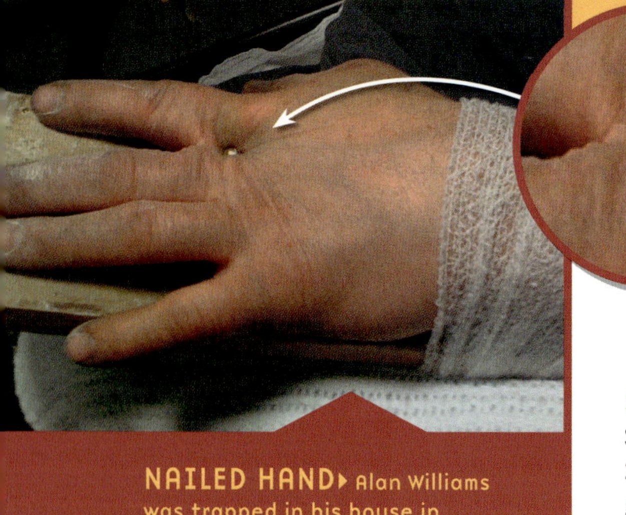

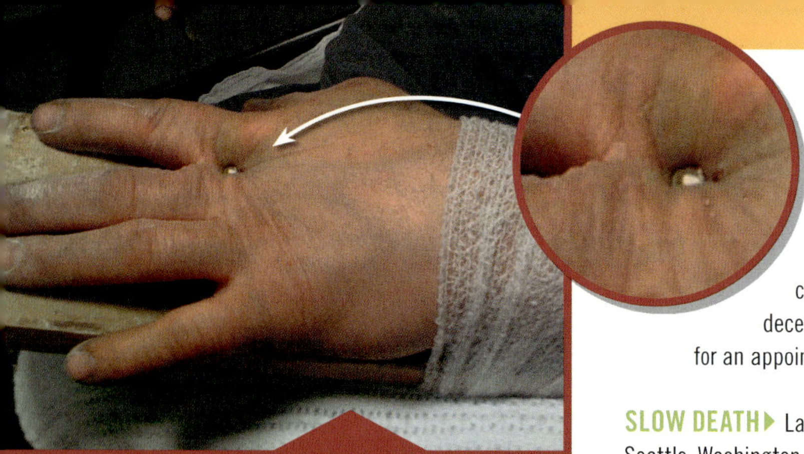

NAILED HAND Alan Williams was trapped in his house in Shropshire, England, for nearly four hours after accidentally nailing himself to the floor. He was doing home improvements when he slipped at the top of the stairs and fired a high-powered 5-in (12.5-cm) bolt through his left hand. Pinned to the floor, he was unable to move or get help until his partner came home. He was then taken to hospital still attached to the floorboard, but luckily the nail missed vital tendons and veins, allowing him to regain full use of his hand.

LATE GUESTS The Lastel Hotel in Tokyo, Japan, caters only to dead clients. Families check in their deceased relatives while waiting for an appointment at a crematorium.

SLOW DEATH Lakeesha LaShawn Johnson of Seattle, Washington State, died on November 4, 2011. Her death was ruled a homicide owing to a gunshot wound she had received 13 years before.

ASH AMMO Instead of having their ashes scattered in the traditional way when they die, hunters can have them turned into ammunition. Alabama company Holy Smoke puts cremated ash into live shells or cartridges—1 lb (2.2 kg) of ash is enough for 250 shells—which can then be loaded into shotguns and fired into the sky at birds or clay targets.

GOLD COINS In February 2012, workers on a building renovation in Les Riceys, France, found a hidden stash of U.S. minted gold coins dating back to the 1850s and worth nearly $1 million.

SHORT CUT Runner Rob Sloan from Sunderland, England, was stripped of his third-place bronze medal in the 2011 Kielder Marathon after he was found to have traveled part of the last 6 mi (9.6 km) of the race by bus.

STILL ALIVE An 87-year-old Swedish woman discovered she had been declared dead by the Swedish Tax Agency after a doctor accidentally wrote her birth details into a death certificate. Although she called the authorities to say she was still very much alive, she was refused her prescription at the local pharmacy as their records stated that she was in fact a "non-existing person."

DENTIST DASH Kurt Wagner from Mödling, Austria, drove 40 mi (64 km) the wrong way down the country's busiest highway, causing at least one accident and a major police operation—because he had a toothache and desperately needed to see a dentist. When arrested, he said he could remember nothing about the drive because he had taken a cocktail of strong medication and alcohol to numb the pain.

VANISHING ACTS

For his book* Vanishing Act, *American photographer Art Wolfe captured a series of amazing shots of wildlife creatures perfectly camouflaged in their natural habitat. Can you spot a wolf peering out from behind a tree in a Montana forest (far right)? Or the giraffe in South Africa that blends in vertically with the shape and color of its surrounding vegetation (right)? And how about the great gray owl in the picture below, taken in Oregon?

COFFIN THERAPY Coffin-maker Stepan Piryanyk, from Truskavets, Ukraine, helps people prepare themselves for the afterlife by allowing them to lie in a casket for 15 minutes in what he calls "coffin therapy." Clients relax to a soothing soundtrack of birdsong and falling water. Putting the lid on is optional.

GARDEN TRENCH To re-create the conditions faced by soldiers during World War I, historian Andrew Robertshaw excavated a 65-ft-long (20-m) trench in the back garden of his home in Surrey, England. It took volunteers about a month to remove the 220 tons of earth needed to make way for an authentic kitchen, infantry bedroom, and officer's dugout.

BACK TO HER ROOTS Since 2008, Val Theroux has made an annual 9,000-mi (14,500-km) round trip from Canada to England—just to see a tree. The retired nurse from Kamloops, British Columbia, fell in love with the oak tree in Hampshire's New Forest while visiting her daughter and became so infatuated with it that she even tracked it down on Google Earth so she could see it from Canada. On her visits, she gets up early in the morning to be alone with the tree, then hugs it and admires it for a few hours. She says: "Some trees will not give you the time of day, while others are very welcoming. I get a lot of healing from this tree and go away feeling like I've seen an old friend."

EXPLODING AQUARIUM Shoppers fled in terror after a shark-filled aquarium suddenly burst open in a busy Dongfang, China, shopping mall, flooding the floor and showering people with flying glass and fish. Fifteen people were injured and three lemon sharks and dozens of smaller fish and turtles perished when the 10-in-thick (25-cm) protective glass of the huge 37-ton tank shattered without warning.

CLEAN EATING The larva of the emerald cockroach wasp disinfects its food before eating. The parasitic larva, which lives inside a cockroach, creates a clear liquid disinfectant solution in its mouth and then spits it out, covering the insides of its host. The disinfectant removes a common cockroach bacterium that is especially deadly to the wasp.

HUMAN TAIL Japanese inventor Shota Ishiwatari has invented a tail for humans, which wags when the wearer is excited. The "Tailly" is attached to a belt that monitors the wearer's pulse. The faster the pulse, the faster the wagging.

LOBSTER BOY

Grady Stiles from Pittsburgh, Pennsylvania, was born in 1937 with two clawlike fingers on each hand and deformed legs. He was the sixth member of his family to be born with the congenital condition ectrodactyly, where the fingers and toes fuse together. In the 1940s he began appearing in circus sideshows with his family, and became known as the "Lobster Boy," a role he performed for almost 50 years.

HOPPING MAD A burglar who broke into a house in Plymouth, England, was caught out after coming face-to-face with the family's giant pet rabbit. Weighing 10 lb (4.5 kg), and measuring 2 ft (60 cm) long, Toby stomped so loudly on the floor of his cage that the intruder panicked and fled.

LENNON CRIMEWAVE Police in Belo Horizonte, Brazil, arrested three John Lennons in January 2013, while a fourth ended up in the city morgue, after allegedly being murdered. The Beatles were hugely popular in Brazil and hundreds of parents named their sons after John Lennon.

DRUNKEN BEASTS

- A black bear passed out on the lawn of a resort in Baker Lake, Washington, in 2004 after drinking 36 cans of beer.
- A gang of drunken monkeys rampaged through an Indian village in 2005 after stealing potent liquor that had been carefully stored in pots for a religious festival.
- A horse in Romania tested positive for alcohol in 2008 after the cart it was pulling hit an elderly man who was sitting on a bench. Ion Dragan had just bought the horse, which may have been given liquor by its previous owners to make it look strong and healthy before being sold.
- Drunk on a fermented-rice-based liquor being prepared for a local festival, a herd of 70 elephants went on a four-day rampage in eastern India in 2010, killing three people and destroying 60 homes.
- In 2011, a number of parrots in Palmerston, Australia, began behaving raucously and falling over after getting drunk as a result of eating alcoholic plants.
- A herd of cows gate-crashed an outdoor party in Boxford, Massachusetts, in 2012 and began drinking the beer that the fleeing partygoers had left behind.

DRUNKEN MOOSE

Per Johansson of Särö, Sweden, arrived home from work to find a drunken moose stuck in his neighbor's tree. In autumn, moose eat fallen, fermented apples, which make them intoxicated. This animal tried to climb into the tree to reach an apple but it became stuck with one hoof on the ground and the other three up the tree. Eventually freed by firefighters, the moose stumbled away from the tree, collapsed on the ground, and went to sleep. Having sobered up overnight, it got up and walked slowly off the next morning.

CHAIR RAGE A male passenger in Torbay, Devon, England, was caught on camera causing £200 ($300) of damage to a bus seat by chewing it.

NUMBERED HEADS Tan Chaoyun of Shenzhen, China, the mother of six-year-old identical quadruplet boys, shaved the numbers 1, 2, 3, and 4 into her sons' heads so that people could tell them apart at school.

BIRTHDAY BLUES As a birthday treat, Xiao Li bought girlfriend Wang Xue a $750 necklace and hid it in a cake—but then could only watch in horror as she wolfed the cake down whole and swallowed the necklace. She subsequently underwent endoscopic surgery in Qingdao, China, where a probe was passed down her throat and into her stomach to retrieve the necklace.

BODY BLOW Owing to severe overcrowding, the dead must be removed after six years from Hong Kong's public cemeteries.

DEAD LOAD When a pickup truck overturned on the highway in Luozhou, China, 16 bodies tumbled out onto the tarmac. Police thought they were investigating a serial killer until it emerged that the driver was a professor from the city's medical school who had bought the corpses of unclaimed murder victims for his students to use in class.

FISH ALERT Emergency services rushed to a suburb of Stockholm, Sweden, to investigate a reported gas leak, but when they arrived they found the smell was nothing more dangerous than fermented herring, a traditional Swedish delicacy.

POLICEMAN STOLEN A life-size cardboard police officer that was being used to reduce crime was stolen from a supermarket in Barnsley, England. The 6-ft-tall (1.8-m) figure, named P.C. Bobb, had been placed in the store to deter shoplifters.

GATOR PARTIES Reptile expert Bob Barrett from Tampa Bay, Florida, provides live alligators for children's pool parties. For $175, he takes an alligator, with its mouth taped shut, to people's backyard pools so that children can swim with it.

KILLER MOOSE In 2009, Ingemar Westlund of Loftahammar, Sweden, was arrested as a murder suspect in the death of his wife—but police released him when it was discovered that she had been killed by a drunken moose.

SYNCHRONIZED FLUSHING To help clear toilet waste that had accumulated in the city's sewers during days of water outages in September 2012, all residents of Bulawayo, Zimbabwe, were urged to flush their toilets simultaneously at 7.30 p.m. twice a week on Mondays and Thursdays.

KING TRUCKER Some historians believe the rightful King of England died in 2012—at a modest house in Jerilderie in New South Wales, Australia. Researchers claimed that Australian forklift truck driver Michael Hastings's ancestors were cheated out of the English crown in the 15th century.

DOUBLE PUNISHMENT When trying to feed a fish to a 9-ft-long (2.7-m) alligator, Florida airboat captain Wallace Weatherholt had his hand bitten off and was subsequently charged with unlawfully feeding the reptile. His hand was found, but could not be reattached.

BIRD'S EYE VIEW Italian tourist Nathalie Rollandin got a bird's eye view of San Francisco Bay—thanks to a greedy seagull. She had been photographing the Golden Gate Bridge when the seagull mistook her camera for food and snatched it while it was still filming. The bird flew off, but soon dropped the camera nearby, leaving behind 30 seconds of unique views of the bay at sunset.

DOUBLE LIFE In the United States, Isaac Osei owns a New York taxi company—but in Ghana, he is royalty. He is the chief of five towns, wears a crown, sits on a throne, and lives in a palace.

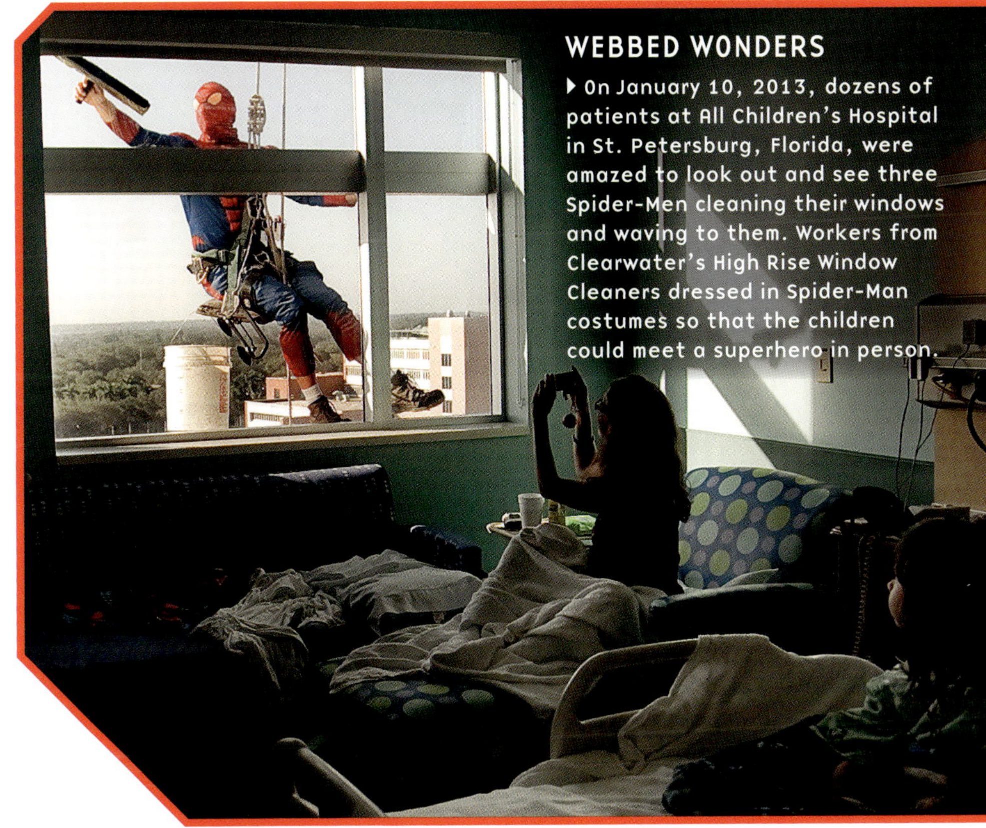

WEBBED WONDERS

On January 10, 2013, dozens of patients at All Children's Hospital in St. Petersburg, Florida, were amazed to look out and see three Spider-Men cleaning their windows and waving to them. Workers from Clearwater's High Rise Window Cleaners dressed in Spider-Man costumes so that the children could meet a superhero in person.

OLDEST NEWLYWEDS After dating for 18 years, of which 15 had been spent living together, 95-year-old Lillian Hartley and 98-year-old Allan Marks finally married in 2012 near their home in Palm Springs, California, to become the world's oldest bride and groom with a combined age of 193 years.

WIPED OUT Since brown tree snakes mysteriously made their way to the Pacific island of Guam in the 1940s, their numbers have grown to two million and they have driven nearly all the island's native birds to the brink of extinction.

PRISON BREAK-IN Police in Sacramento, California, arrested parolee Marvin Lane Ussery for attempting to break into Folsom Prison—from where he had been released two years earlier.

LICKED BOTTOM

Zhang Bangsheng, a devoted keeper at Wuhan Zoo, China, saved the life of a rare three-month-old Francois' langur monkey by licking its bottom for an hour to encourage it to defecate. He had noticed that the monkey had eaten a peanut and was in pain through being unable to pass it. As the monkey was too young to be given laxatives, Zhang cleaned its bottom with warm water and started licking. He was soon rewarded when the constipated monkey successfully passed the peanut.

BRIDE AND GROOM Retired schoolteacher Liu Fu from Zhengzhou, China, finally posed for her wedding pictures 30 years after her husband died. She played both the bride and groom in the glamorous photos, staged with the help of wardrobe experts, hairdressers, and makeup artists. When she and husband Feng had married, they were short of money, but she had always wanted a proper wedding album.

NEIGHBORHOOD NINJA Ken Andre, a volunteer Neighborhood Watch member, patrols the streets of Yeovil in Somerset, England, dressed as a ninja. The martial arts expert and father-of-two, also known as "Shadow," dons black Japanese robes to combat crime and has foiled dozens of street attacks.

CLOWN DOCTORS Proving that laughter is the best medicine, Professor Thomas Petschner and Rita Noetzel founded Clown Doctors of New Zealand to promote the medical use of clowns in hospitals across the country. The Clown Doctors also donned their red noses and costumes to perform when a massive earthquake struck Christchurch. They spent weeks bringing light relief to the rescue teams.

ZOMBIE STORE The Zombie Apocalypse store in Las Vegas, Nevada, sells a range of items for dealing with the undead, including 3-D bleeding ex-girlfriend zombie targets and Tasers disguised as cell phones.

DEAD CANDIDATES At the 2012 U.S. elections, voters elected two dead politicians to represent them. Earl K. Wood, a Democrat standing in Orlando, Florida, and Alabama Republican Charles Beasley both recorded convincing victories despite having died weeks before polling took place.

SNOT NICE! Yuk! This silicone, novelty nose-shaped dispenser squirts green shower gel through the nostrils to re-create the essence of fresh mucus from a really heavy cold.

DRESSED CRAB

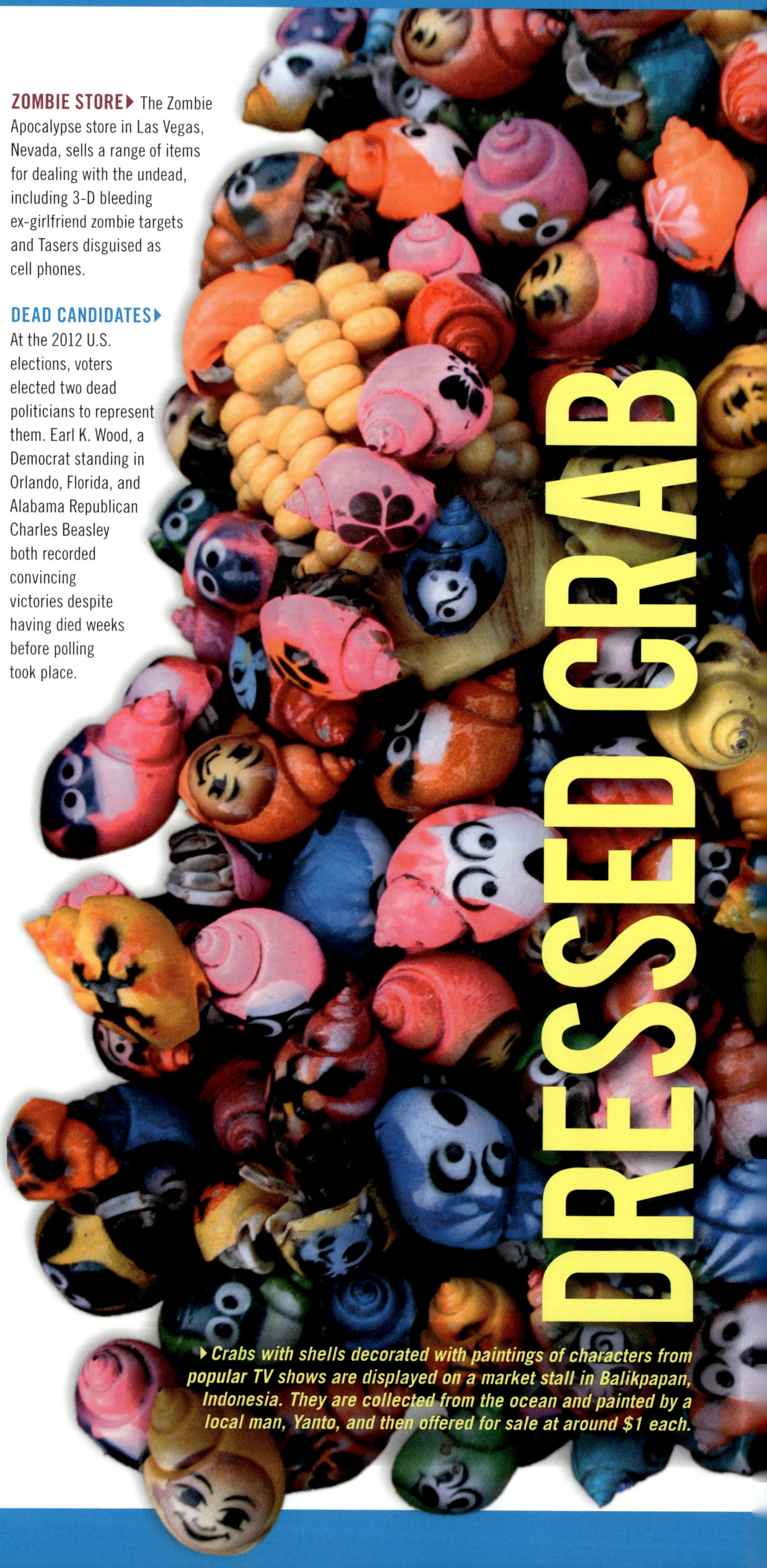

Crabs with shells decorated with paintings of characters from popular TV shows are displayed on a market stall in Balikpapan, Indonesia. They are collected from the ocean and painted by a local man, Yanto, and then offered for sale at around $1 each.

UNINVITED CLEANER A woman broke into a house in Westlake, Ohio, took out the garbage, vacuumed the carpet, washed some dishes, and tidied up the living room, then left the home owners a bill for $75 written on a napkin.

EVA'S TRAVELS In 1955, three years after her death, the embalmed corpse of Argentina's First Lady Eva Peron was snatched—and it then went on a global trek for two decades. In turn it was kept in a van, behind a cinema screen in Buenos Aires, and then inside the city's waterworks. After being secretly transported to Italy and buried under a false name, it was disinterred and taken to Spain before finally returning to Buenos Aires, where it now lies 16.4 ft (5 m) underground in La Recoleta Cemetery in a heavily fortified crypt.

EVERY YEAR ABOUT 1.8 MILLION SHOPPING CARTS ARE STOLEN OR LOST IN THE UNITED STATES.

CHEESE GAS A road tunnel in northern Norway was closed for three weeks after a truck's cargo of 27 tons of caramelized brown goat cheese caught fire. Trapped in the tunnel, the cheese continued to burn for days, releasing potentially lethal gases.

TUTAN-ALAN Following his death in 2011, Alan Billis from Devon, England, was mummified in the style of the Ancient Egyptians. After he had responded to a newspaper advert looking for someone to become a mummy, scientists at the University of York devised techniques to embalm his body using Ancient Egyptian methods. He could now remain preserved in his mummified state for 3,000 years!

MAZE MISERY A family became so scared and disoriented while wandering around a cornfield maze in Danvers, Massachusetts, that they called emergency services for a rescue. They entered the spooky 7-acre (2.8-ha) maze, which was cut in the shape of a headless horseman, by daylight but panicked when night fell.

SUPER NAMES Two men from Nottingham, England, officially changed their names to consist of 15 superhero or super-villain names each. Daniel Knox-Hewson became Emperor Spiderman Gandalf Wolverine Skywalker Optimus Prime Goku Sonic Xavier Ryu Cloud Superman Heman Batman Thrash, while Kelvin Borbridge opted for Baron Venom Balrog Sabretooth Vader Megatron Vegeta Robotnik Magneto Bison Sephiroth Lex Luthor Skeletor Joker Grind.

HANGING AROUND

Suspension artist Deana Brown spent eight hours hanging like a piece of meat from the ceiling of a room in Baltimore, Maryland, by huge metal hooks inserted into the skin of her shoulders.

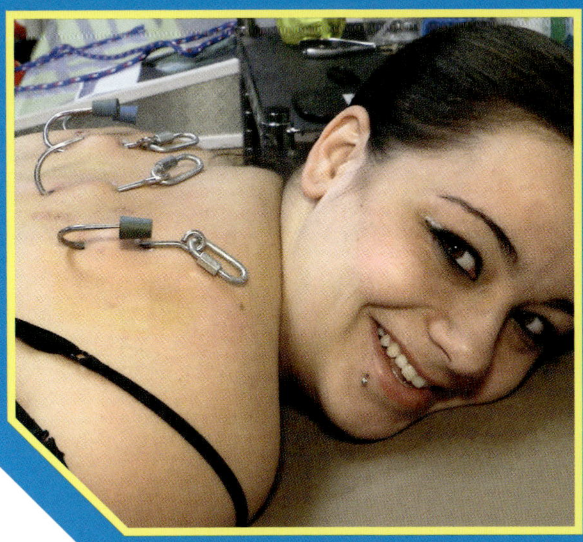

"When I'm suspended from hooks it feels like an enlightenment—when I do it I feel as if I'm free. It's also a great back stretcher and it's amazing to feel free even though you're hooked up like a piece of meat."

INVISIBLE MAN In February 2012, paramedics and a deputy sheriff responded to a call from a 28-year-old man from Winder, Georgia, who had phoned 911 to report that he was invisible.

NAKED AMBITION Eager to escape the rat race, Masafumi Nagasaki, 79, has been living naked as the sole inhabitant of the Japanese desert island of Sotobanari for more than 20 years. The only time he puts on clothes is when he makes his weekly trip to a nearby island to collect water and rice cakes.

HIDDEN SNAKES A man was arrested on suspicion of stealing five exotic snakes from a pet store in Mesa, Arizona, by hiding them down his shorts for more than an hour.

LIZARD KING Businessman Tyler Gold of York, Nebraska, legally changed his name to Tyrannosaurus Rex in 2012 because he thought it was cooler than his real name. His full legal name is Tyrannosaurus Rex Joseph Gold.

DISNEY WEDDING Jason Webb-Flint and his wife Julie celebrated 20 years of marriage by renewing their wedding vows dressed as Mickey and Minnie Mouse. All the guests at the wedding in Kent, England, turned up as Disney characters, with the couple's teenaged sons attending as Donald Duck and Goofy and no fewer than four people dressing up as Pocahontas. Disney songs including "Colonel Hathi's March" from *The Jungle Book* were played during the service.

Juicy!

CRAZY CARROT

Beatriz van Winden-Guzman, from Holland, found this very odd shaped carrot in her garden! It is one carrot with lots of other carrots growing out of it.

CHICKEN STOLEN A man was arrested after an 8-ft-tall (2.4-m) fiberglass chicken was stolen from a chicken farm in Ontario, Canada. The thief made off with the bird after severing it at the legs.

SECOND ARK Dutch millionaire Johan Huibers built a replica of Noah's Ark—a full-sized vessel measuring 450 ft (137 m) long by 70 ft (21 m) wide. Complete with life-size plastic animals, it was inspired by a dream he had in 1992 in which the Netherlands was flooded by the North Sea. The ark took Johan four years to build.

SARDINE SPILL The highway near Kolobrzeg, Poland, was closed for hours after a truck driver forgot to shut his rear door properly and spilled 26 tons of sardines onto the road.

RODENT'S REVENGE Dale Whitmell of Ontario, Canada, was lucky to escape with his life when he accidentally shot himself in the forehead while trying to kill a mouse with the butt of his rifle. He had not realized the gun was loaded.

POOPER HERO In 2011, a mysterious superhero called SuperVaclav donned a helmet, mask, and tights to patrol the parks of Prague, Czech Republic, and wage war on dog owners who failed to clear up their pets' poops.

LOST BET A 21-year-old man was stuck for nine hours overnight in a park at Vallejo, California, after betting his friends $100 that he could fit into a children's playground swing. With the help of liquid laundry detergent, he managed to slide his legs into the swing, but then he became stuck and his friends vanished. Fire crews cut him free the next morning.

BEST FRIENDS

Anzac the baby kangaroo and Peggy the baby wombat became best friends after the orphaned pair shared a pouch at an animal rescue center in Victoria, Australia. The youngsters constantly huddled together, taking comfort from each other's movement and heartbeat.

PENGUIN CANDIDATE▸ Campaigning while dressed as a penguin, Professor Pongoo (aka Mike Ferrigan) polled 444 votes in the Pentland Hills ward for the City of Edinburgh Council, Scotland, in 2012, thereby receiving more votes than both the Liberal Democrats and the Green Party. If elected, he had promised to attend council meetings in the penguin costume.

TREE TRIBUTE▸ As a tribute to his late wife Janet, who died in 1995, farmer Winston Howes of Gloucestershire, England, planted 6,000 oak trees in a 6-acre (2.4-hectare) field leaving a perfect heart shape in the middle—with the point facing in the direction of her childhood home.

TASTY TAPE▸ A 23-year-old woman from Marietta, Georgia, eats 6,000 ft (1,830 m)—that's more than a mile—of Scotch tape every month. She has been addicted to eating tape for over nine years and goes through three rolls a day, chewing each piece for about 30 seconds before swallowing.

ADDED INTEREST▸ A driver in Sicily was handed a whopping $44,500 fine for illegal parking after an Italian police officer mistakenly added on 1,800 years of interest because he calculated the fine back to the year AD 208 instead of 2008.

DOZY TOURIST▸ Italian security guards checking the baggage at Rome's Fiumicino Airport were alarmed when they spotted on an X-ray a Norwegian tourist curled up fast asleep among the suitcases on the moving belt. The man traveled for around 160 ft (50 m) on the belt before police caught up with him.

MEMORY MAN▸ Community police officer Andy Pope has such an incredible memory for faces that he successfully identified more than 130 wanted people in 12 months on the streets of Birmingham, England, having memorized their images just from CCTV stills. He even recognized a serial robber in the street a whole year after his image had appeared on TV.

BEARDED LADY▸ A woman robbed a bank in Cottondale, Alabama, dressed as a man, completing her disguise with a beard drawn on with a black marker.

SPACE CHICKEN

▸Wearing a knitted spacesuit and helmet, and with a modified lunchbox as a spacecraft, Camilla the rubber chicken floated to the edge of space in March 2012 to test levels of radiation during an intense solar storm. She was launched into space attached to a helium balloon by Bishop Union High School students in California and sent to an altitude of 120,000 ft (36,575 m). Carrying four cameras, a cryogenic thermometer, and two GPS trackers, the chicken spent 90 minutes in the stratosphere before the balloon popped and she parachuted safely back to Earth.

INDEX

Page numbers in italic refer to the illustrations

Ripley's
Believe It or Not!®
www.ripleybooks.com

ACKNOWLEDGMENTS

Cover (l) www.50fifty-gifts.com, (r) Steven Larimer & Cindy Rio; **4** Earth to Sky Calculus/NASA; **6–7** www.idrinkleadpaint.com/twitter @idrinkleadpaint; **8** KeystoneUSA-ZUMA/Rex Features; **9** Gregg Valentino; **10** (sp) Jennifer Dawson (curator) and Vent Haven Museum KY, (b) Tom Ladshaw courtesy of Vent Haven Museum KY; **11** (sp) Jennifer Dawson (curator) and Vent Haven Museum KY, (b) Tom Ladshaw courtesy of Vent Haven Museum KY; **12** Jennifer Dawson (curator) and Vent Haven Museum KY; **13** (t/l, t/r, b/l) Jennifer Dawson (curator) and Vent Haven Museum KY, (b/r) James Kriegsmann/Michael Ochs Archives/Getty Images; **14–15** Jennifer Dawson (curator) and Vent Haven Museum KY; **16** (t) Getty Images, (c/l, b) Jennifer Dawson (curator) and Vent Haven Museum KY; **17** (t/l) Bryan Simon/Jennifer Dawson (curator) Vent Haven Museum KY, (t/r, c, b) Jennifer Dawson (curator) and Vent Haven Museum KY; **18** Caters News; **19** (c, t) AP/Press Association Images, (b) London News Pictures/Rex Features; **20** (b) Alan Sailer/Rex Features, (t/l, t/c, t/r) Steven Larimer & Cindy Rio; **21** (t) Steven Larimer & Cindy Rio, (b) Donald L. Sammons; **22** (t) BNPS, (b) © Mariam A. Montesinos/epa/Corbis; **23** Wes Naman/Rex Features; **24** (t/r) Circus World Museum, Baraboo, Wisconsin, (b) Saskatchewan Archives Board R-A3465; **25** (t/l, b/r) Circus World Museum, Baraboo, Wisconsin; **26** Caters News; **27** Circus World Museum, Baraboo, Wisconsin; **28** Jan Wiriden/GT/Scanpix/Press Association Images; **29** (t/r) © Cherie Diez/Tampa Bay Times/ZumaPress.com/eyevine, (b/r) Quirky China News/Rex Features; **30** (r) Getty Images, (l) www.50fifty-gifts.com; **32** (t) Beatriz van Winden-Guzman, (b) Rob Leeson/Newspix/Rex Features; **33** Earth to Sky Calculus/NASA; **Back cover** Donald L. Sammons

Key: t = top, b = bottom, c = center, l = left, r = right, sp = single page, dp = double page

All other photos are from Ripley Entertainment Inc.
Every attempt has been made to acknowledge correctly and contact copyright holders and we apologize in advance for any unintentional errors or omissions, which will be corrected in future editions.